The Oxford Piano Method

P·I·A·N·O T·I·M·E

GOING PLACES

Pauline Hall and *Korky Paul*

MUSIC DEPARTMENT

OXFORD
UNIVERSITY PRESS

OXFORD
UNIVERSITY PRESS

Great Clarendon Street, Oxford OX2 6DP, England
198 Madison Avenue, New York, NY10016, USA

Oxford University Press is a department of the University of Oxford.
It furthers the University's aim of excellence in research, scholarship,
and education by publishing worldwide

Oxford is a registered trade mark of Oxford University Press
in the UK and in certain other countries

22

ISBN 978-0-19-372730-4

Music and text origination by
Barnes Music Engraving Ltd., East Sussex
Printed in Great Britain on acid-free paper by
Halstan & Co. Ltd., Amersham, Bucks.

Contents

Beep! beep!

Imagine you are beeping your horn at someone and are getting quite angry. Really jab at those left hand cross-over notes!

Fiona Macardle

Treading carefully

Alan Haughton

Balloon ride

Roderick Skeaping

Gent - ly blow - ing, light - ly flow - ing in our hot air bal - loon. Clouds un - fold - ing, slow - ly mould - ing shapes ris - ing like mon - sters in the sky so high.

Michael, row the boat ashore

American folk tune

On the move

Mich - ael, row the boat a - shore, Hal - le - lu -

mf

- jah, Mich-ael, row the boat a - shore, Hal - le - lu - jah. Sis - ter,

f

help to trim the sail, Hal - le - lu - jah, sis - ter, help to trim the

Slower

sail, Hal - le - lu - jah. *mp*

p

Cossack dance

Denis McCaldin

Hong Kong ferry

There are no white keys in this piece,
so keep your hands well up over the black keys.

Pauline Hall

Take a walk

Alan Haughton

Hop it!

Not too fast

Alan Haughton

Flannagan's jig

Alan Haughton

Bluemerang

To Australia and back

Alan Haughton

Mission in space

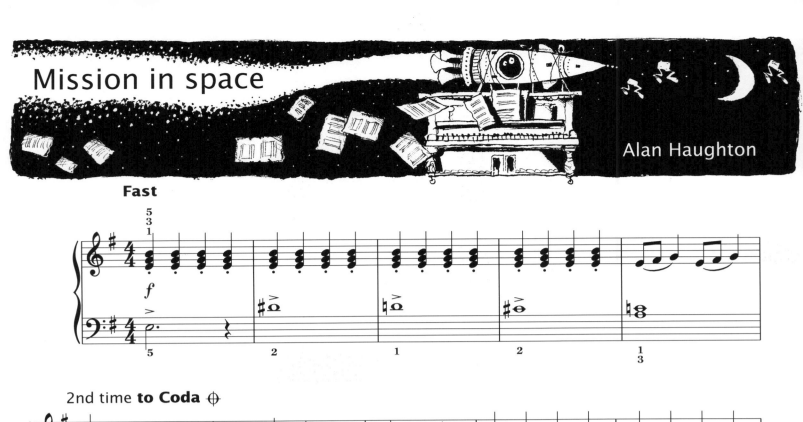

Alan Haughton

Fast

2nd time **to Coda** ⊕

D.C. al Coda   ⊕ **CODA**

Contrary motion in space and time!

There are only black keys here, so keep your fingers ready to play them!

Slow and steady

Roderick Skeaping

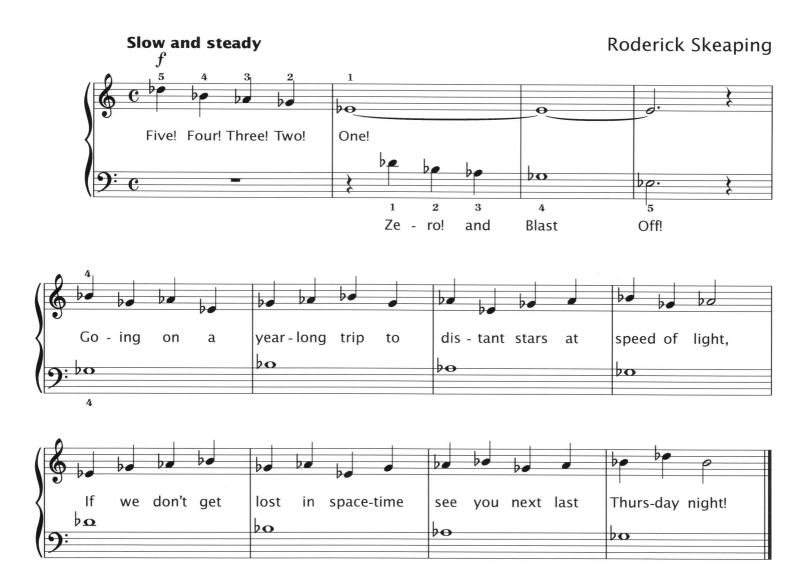

Flying above the clouds

Alan Bullard

Graceful and dreamy

Let sleeping sharks lie

David Cullen

Cycle ride

Mark Andrews

Rollerblade rag

Alan Haughton

Chopsticks with a twist

Fiona Macardle

As fast as possible, with heavy accents where marked

Honk! honk!

With energy

Roderick Skeaping

Cars and lor-ries | in the high street | Toot! toot! | Beep! beep!

An - y-where! but | NOT IN MY STREET! | Don't drive! | Use feet!

Penny-farthing

Tempo di minuetto ($\bm{\s). } = c.56$)

Alan Bullard

A swim in crocodile river

David Cullen

Mexican march

David Cullen

Moderato (♩ = 112)

Paris promenade

David Cullen

The train

Roderick Skeaping

sempre f　　　　　　　　　　**rall.**

Dri - ver sees the sig - nal low - er;　pulls the brake: 'She's get - ting slow - er!'

Ped. _____

Grinding to a halt . . .

Till she stops in - side the sta - tion,　on her way a - cross the na - tion.

a tempo　　　　　　　　　　　　　　　　*lunga*

Woooo!　　　　Woooo!　　　　　　*pp*

Ped. _____　　*Ped.* _____　　*Ped.* _____

Santa Lucia
Italian song

Pauline Hall

Slow waltz time

p smoothly　　　　　　　　　　　　　　　*simile*

mf

New Orleans

David Cullen

Allegro (♩ = 132)

rall.

The bluebottle's last journey

S. Watt

Cautiously

Two in tandem

Primo right hand an octave higher throughout.

Alan Bullard